NEW YORK

New York Souvenir Company

The Chrysler Building, Empire State Building and the *World Trade Center* stand tall above the urban center called Manhattan.

The skyline is familiar two identical towers, rising amid a sea of office buildings. The photographs conjure up sounds of hustle and bustle, images of grandeur, and feelings of excitement. The picture is familiar, even to those who have never been there. It's unmistakably **New York**, the most visited city in the world, though it wasn't always so.

In the year 1609 at the height of the Age of Discovery the English explorer **Henry Hudson** came searching for a sea route to the Orient. He entered the river which now bears his name and there in the mouth of this river lay a 12-mile-long island the Indians called Manhattan. Hudson's sponsors the Dutch, eyed this strategic location as a possible colony.

Dutch settlers arrived in 1624, and within two years they had purchased the island from the Indians for the equivalent of twenty four dollars. In a city where billions of dollars in real estate change hands every year, that transaction remains the most famous deal of all time. Over the next fifty years ownership of the property would change hands several times between the **Dutch** - who called it **New Amsterdam**- and the **British** who named it **New York**, after the Duke of York, brother of then King Charles II.

*The twin-towered **World Trade Center** remains the tallest building in Manhattan.* ➤

*The night skyline of **New York** shimmering on the Hudson River.*

Great Britain claimed **New York** for more than a century, including the time of the Revolutionary War and for years after the signing of the Declaration of Independence. Finally, in 1783, with the signing of the Treaty of Paris, the last British troops left the city. A year later

New York, with its 33,000 inhabitants, was universally recognized as the capital of the **United States of America**. Though that distinction would last only six years, **New York City** had already become the heart of American business. By 1898, the population of Greater New York

had exploded to 3.4-million, making it the second largest city in the world. Today, the **World Trade Center** and the **Empire State building** tower over the skyline of **New York City**, home to more than 7 million and at once the world's hub of trade, finance, the arts, publishing, entertainment, sports and tourism. 23 million visitors explore the city each year, seeing a vibrancy and vitality that those first Dutch settlers never could have imagined when they set up camp on an island called "**Manhattan**".

The construction of **The Empire State Building**, completed during the Great Depression, was a defining event in New York's coming of age as a truly great city of the 20th century.

Although it took only two years to complete, another 12 years passed before the office space was leased to capacity. Like everywhere else in the world, New York was financially crippled by the Depression.

Soaring 1,250 feet above Fifth Avenue in midtown Manhattan, the **Empire State Building** is the world's quintessential skyscraper, affording on a clear day, a view of fifty miles from the 102nd floor observation deck.

During the peak of its construction, the building proceeded at a record pace of four-and-a-half stories per week. It took only two years to build, but due to the depression - more than a dozen years passed before all its office space was occupied. The "Empty State Building", as New Yorkers had come to call it, already had a storied history. It is frequently struck by lightning, and in 1945 an Army B-25 aircraft crashed into the 79th floor, killing 14 and causing $1-million damage.

Spotlight illumination of the upper floors ensures that nobody can miss this majestic structure in the dark of night.

*The **Statue of Liberty** atop her pedestal on **Liberty Island**.*

Statue of Liberty, she stands alone on an island less than two miles from the southern tip of Manhattan. Lady Liberty, facing out to sea with New Jersey at her back, holds a golden torch aloft welcoming ships to the friendly shores of America. Indeed, for decades, shiploads of immigrants from all over the world passed before her gaze moments before landing at **Ellis Island** and entering their adopted country. The **Statue of Liberty** was a gift from the people of France in 1886 to commemorate an alliance that dates back to the American Revolution. At age ninety Lady Liberty received a "makeover" of sorts. Scaffolding was erected around the statue to enable workers to finish a complete restoration in time for the U.S. Bicentennial, in 1976. Every day, visitors take a scenic boat cruise from Battery Park to Liberty Island, followed by an elevator ride from the base of the statue to an observation deck. A further 162 steps lead up into the crown atop the statue's head for a remarkable view of Manhattan and New York Harbor.

The **Statue of Liberty** *has a 3' mouth and a 35' waist making her a grand dame indeed.*

Ellis Island

If the **Statue of Liberty** is the first historic site to visit, for many the second is **Ellis Island**, located just off Battery Park, at the south end of Manhattan. From 1892 to 1954, between twelve and sixteen million immigrants first set foot on American soil at the Ellis Island Immigration Center. Completely renovated and reopened in 1990, Ellis Island is now a museum to the American immigrant and a major tourist attraction.

Battery Park's *esplanade overlooks New York's spectacular harbor.*

*The **Fraunces Tavern** where **George Washington** bid farewell to his officers in 1783.*

Battery Park is itself an historic site; named for its battery of cannon which defended the early settlements, it's an oasis of green space for present-day financial district lunchers and tourists en route to the **Statue of Liberty**.

Also in the neighborhood in a park of its own is **New York's** surprisingly small but elegant **City Hall**. Taking from 1802 to 1811 to build with numerous construction problems, it is still one of America's most impressive city halls. Between the two parks, **Fraunces Tavern**, while not a government building or a revolutionary fort, was the bar where in 1783 **George Washington** bid farewell to his officers before heading south to bolster the government of the nascent republic.

*New York's small but impressive **City Hall** in City Hall Park.*

Prometheus overlooking Rockefeller Center's summertime outdoor restaurant.

In 1938, after seven years of construction, **Rockefeller Center** pushed New York's financial district north to 50th St. in midtown Manhattan. A true masterpiece of functional architecture located around 5th Avenue, the Center integrates huge towers with lush gardens, a pedestrian promenade, concert hall, cinema, underground shops and restaurants, and direct access to the subway. In a sea of concrete office buildings, Rockefeller Center stands alone as a people-friendly place for both workers and tourists.

At 70 stories, the **General Electric building** is the tallest of the many structures that comprise Rockefeller Center, and is home to the studios of **NBC** and the famous rooftop restaurant, "**Rainbow and Stars**".

Those who visit early in the Christmas season often mingle with New Yorkers for the traditional Christmas tree lighting festivities at the base of **Prometheus' Statue**. The tree, the music, the throngs of skaters and well wishers make New York's Christmas season one of the warmest and most exciting in the world.

*Flags from every country in the world surround the plaza at **Rockefeller Center**.* ➤

*The 70-story **G.E. building** towers over Rockefeller Center.*

*Skaters enjoying the ice time at **New York's** most popular rink in the heart of **Rockefeller Center.***

Access to the plaza is gained via Channel Gardens, a mini-boulevard of fountains, statuary and floral decorations between two rows of exclusive shops. During holiday season the gardens are transformed into a winter wonderland of sculpted angels. Just around the corner a statue of Atlas labors under an iron globe with signs of the zodiac.

Seasonal display in **Channel Gardens** *at Rockefeller Center.*

Atlas holding the world high on New York's busy **Fifth Avenue.**

From **Chrysler** to **Rockefeller** to **Trump**, many of New York's big names have one thing in common: skyscrapers. Since the first one popped up in lower Manhattan in 1890, the city's skyline has been in a continuous state of change. For decades each succeeding generation seemed to outdo its predecessor in re-defining the city scene. And, while New York is often first thought of in terms of its tallest buildings, some of the most interesting "sky-scrapers" can be found among the oldest and more diminutive. **The Flatiron building** appeared in 1902 on a narrow triangle of real estate where Broadway crosses 5th Avenue and 23rd Street. Faced with one of the city's toughest architectural challenges, the developer produced a distinctive wedge-shaped building that remains an eye-pleaser to this day.

*Aerial view of **Manhattan** with **New Jersey** across the **Hudson River**.* ➤

By 1930 the race was on to build the tallest skyscraper. **The Chrysler Building**, with its stainless steel spire, was the early winner. To this day it remains a sentimental favorite among native New Yorkers, but within a year the Chrysler Building had been surpassed by the completion of the **Empire State Building**, which held the title for 45 years. Then the **World Trade Center** with twin towers reaching 1350 feet into the sky topped its nearest contender by 100 feet.

Bigger was no longer necessarily better by the late 1970's however, as evidenced by the appearance of post-modern architecture in the peaked **Citicorp bank building** and the bronzed-glass **Trump Tower**, which brought flashy opulence to the forefront of contemporary New York. Trump's multi-level shopping mall features swaths of rose marble, brass and glass skylights and an eighty foot waterfall.

*The **World Trade Center** rising above the financial district.*

*The **U.N.** and skyscrapers of mid-town Manhattan including the **Empire State Building** and the **Chrysler Building**.*

*The distinctive shape of the **Citicorp Building**.*

*The **New York Stock Exchange** offers tours daily.*

*The **Metlife Building** on Park Avenue.*

The mood and pulse of New York are sensed along the avenues and streets of Manhattan. Perhaps the city's most famous boulevard is **Park Avenue**. On a winter's night decorative lights bounce off the slick pavement as automobiles streak by, while on a spring afternoon tulips provide a splash of cheerful color against the urgent walls of this urban canyon. At the south end of the boulevard stands the imposing **MetLife Building**, known previously as the **PanAm Building**.

The potential chaos of a normal day's street traffic is controlled by a logical grid system of mostly one-way numbered streets and avenues. However, anyone who has dared drive a car in Manhattan can testify that there are many exceptions to the rules. As one drives south from midtown into **Greenwich Village**, numbered streets are gradually replaced by streets with names. And, the grid system disappears completely downtown where the original plan was designed for horses, carts and pedestrians.

If one were to choose a "Main Street" for New York it would likely be **Broadway**. Besides being world-famous for theater, Broadway is unique as the only thoroughfare to run the entire twelve miles of Manhattan from its northern tip to Battery Park at the sound end.

*A view of **5th Avenue** with the **Empire State Building** in the distance*

Park Avenue reflects Christmas lights and street lamps at night.

The buildings of **Upper West Side** *in winter.*

Bleecker Street, *in the heart of Greenwich Village.*

*"**The Dakota**" apartment building, once home to* John Lennon, *is situated on West 72nd St., across the road from Central Park.*

*Broadway and 7th Avenue intersect as seen from **Times Square**. Broadway bends to the southeast while 7th Avenue runs straight south.*

*The narrow streets of **Little Italy**, decorated for the annual Italian festival.*

*An aerial view of the **United Nations** with the East River and 59th St. Bridge in the background and the East Side residential area to the left.*

What may be the world's most important meeting place, **The United Nations**, is situated on 18 acres of **East River** waterfront between 42nd and 48th Streets and 1st Avenue. This vast working monument to world peace and international diplomacy is one of the three most-visited attractions in New York, after the Statue of Liberty and Central Park. Each year nearly a million tourists shuffle through United Nations plaza and gardens. Guided tours are offered in thirty languages, and visitors can rub shoulders with diplomats in the U.N. Delegates' Dining Room.

*The U.N.'s chief landmark, the tall **Secretariat Building**.*

The most recognizable structure at the U.N. is the **Secretariat Building**, a 544 ft. green-glass slab set between narrow end walls of white marble. But, it is the lower profile **General Assembly Building**, which provides the setting for meetings of the member nations whose flags decorate the perimeter of the complex. The General Assembly provides seating for 1,400 delegates, 160 journalists, and 400 visitors. Through earphones at their seats delegates may listen to speeches, translated into one of the six official languages of the assembly: English, Russian, Chinese, French, Spanish or Arabic.

The Secretariat Building is next to the curved, low profile General Assembly Building.

The interior of the General Assembly Hall.

While the ornate towers, domes and spires of churches often dominate the skylines of other major cities, in New York a forest of skyscrapers can be overlooked. But that would be a mistake for any visitor because the churches, temples and synagogues of New York are no less impressive than their cousins around the world.

In all it's splendor, the **Cathedral Church of St. John The Divine** stands an incomplete project, more than a century after the foundation was laid. But even in unfinished state, St. John's is the largest gothic cathedral in the world with 121,000 square feet of floor area. Among its myriad features are four doors of solid Burmese teak and one of bronze. Another of the largest places of worship in the city is **Temple Emanu-El**, a Romanesque synagogue on 5th Avenue, overlooking Central Park. The largest Roman Catholic cathedral in America, **St. Patrick's** also on 5th Avenue, stands as a symbol of New York's early Irish Catholic immigrant population.

The Cathedral Church of St. John the Divine.

The Gothic-style spires of St. Patrick's Cathedral. ❯

Temple Emanu-El is the largest reform synagogue in the United States.

*The front steps of the **Metropolitan Museum of Art** are a popular resting place for weary museum goers and passersby.*

The Solomon R. Guggenheim Museum *houses a collection of 4,000 paintings, sculptures and drawings from the Impressionist period to the present.*

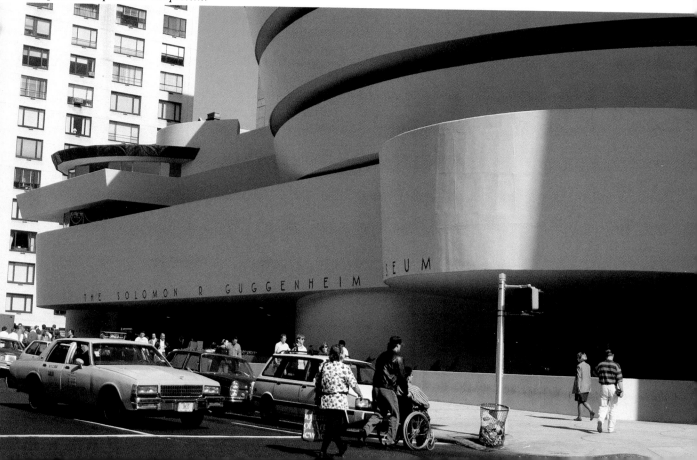

*The collections of the **Museum of Natural History** trace the history of the world from the age of dinosaurs to the space age.*

***The Cloisters Museum of Medieval Art and Architecture,** situated in Fort Tryon park at the northern tip of Manhattan.*

In numbers and variety the museums of New York seem to overpower the imaginations of the millions who visit them each year. There are entire museums dedicated to children, toys, police, broadcasting, coin collecting, computers and many other, more obscure pursuits. Art galleries alone number more than four hundred, the largest of which is the **Metropolitan Museum of Art**. The "Met" collection, spanning the entire history of artistic expression, is the centerpiece of "**Museum Mile**", a veritable community of world class galleries extending along the eastern side of Central Park and south along 5th Avenue. Further south, the **SoHo district** is noted for its profusion of smaller art galleries where one can stumble upon original works of artists ranging from **Rembrandt** to **Warhol**. Something for every age and taste.

*Stately limousines are never far from the entrance to the **Plaza Hotel**.*

New York has always been a city of hotels, from the evenings George Washington's rebels bunked in the spartan surroundings of colonial New York, to the late nights **Ernest Hemingway** spent philosophizing in the bar of his favorite hotel on Central Park South. Such varied souls as **Groucho Marx, Eleanor Roosevelt** and **Mark Twain** once haunted the famous **Plaza Hotel**, one of several exclusive inns with a coveted view of Central Park. But, whether up-scale or down and dirty, every hotel in New York has a tale to tell. In the **Chelsea district**, a few run-down hotels are marked with plaques honoring famous writers, artists and musicians whose inspirations came while lodged between their clapboard walls. And of course, there are today's modern hotels; an endless list of the **Sheraton**; the **Hilton**, the **Westin**, the **Marriott**, the **Peninsula**, the **Meridian** and numerous other big names of hospitality, all vying to serve the visitor.

*The **Waldorf Astoria** remains one of the most prestigious hotels in New York, more than one hundred years after it was originally built on the block now occupied by the Empire State Building.* ➤

*From spring through fall, rowboats are available for rent on **Central Park Lake**.*

From outer space the most distinguishing feature of New York city is surely **Central Park**, a green rectangle of 840 acres in area. Its possibilities for a wide variety of leisure activities such as picnicking, rowing or horse and buggy rides make **Central Park** a welcome respite from the never-ending din of daily life.

Central Park extends from 59th St. to 110th St., between 5th Avenue and Central Park West.

Horse-drawn cabs are available at the southeast and southwest corners of Central Park on 59th Street.

The borders of **Central Park** were drawn in 1862, when the northern half of Manhattan was largely undeveloped land. Over the decades residential neighborhoods grew up around the park as it became popular for its beautifully landscaped gardens, tranquil ponds, playgrounds and natural bird sanctuaries. Today, **Central Park** also attracts visitors for outdoor theater, open air concerts, zoos and a host of sports including jogging, cycling, rollerblading, tennis and baseball.

Central Park was designed to make the visitor feel as far away from the city as possible, though one is never more than a quarter mile from the perimeter. The park's designers planted tall trees along ridge lines and made the groves especially dense along the bordering stone walls to foster the illusion. Thirty-two miles of winding footpaths beckon city dwellers to abandon regimented city life and wander for a few minutes or a few hours in a more natural environment.

*City sights and sounds fade out of range at one of **Central Park's** many fountains.*

*Sea lions perch on the rocks at **Central Park Zoo**.*

*A sculpture of **Alice In Wonderland** blends into the bare trees of autumn in **Central Park**.*

*Joggers and cyclists share a warm day on **Central Park Drive**.*

The center of American style and fashion for 150 years, New York attracts shoppers from across the globe. From the trendy designer shops of **Fifth Avenue** to the curbside second-hand dealers of **Greenwich Village**, to the chattering chaos of **Canal St.**, an exciting shopping experience awaits people of any age any budget.

*The largest department store in the world, **Macy's**, on Broadway at Herald Square.*

Long before architects developed a grandiose vision of a city of skyscrapers, a smaller yet equally ambitious genre of artisans left their imprint on New York. They carved statues, erected monuments and designed bell-towers in the European tradition. Look carefully in the parks and squares hidden between the office towers and you'll find monuments to the New York of another era.

The arch at **Washington Square** seems inspired by its cousins in London and Paris. It was built in 1889 to commemorate the Centennial of George Washington's inauguration as the first President of The United States. The original was made of wood and pleased New Yorkers enough to commission its marble successor that remains to this day a **Greenwich Village** landmark.

With Central Park at its back, and 5th Ave. on its flank, the monument to **General William Tecumseh Sherman** seems to be marching across **Grand Army Plaza** toward a triumphal reception at the Plaza Hotel. However outlandish a scenario that would be today, in 1903 it was entirely appropriate. The statue, covered in gold leaf, commemorates General Sherman's substantial feats during the Civil War.

*The **Bell Statue** at Herald Square.*

*Monument to **Ulysses S. Grant**.*

*Gold Statue in honor of **General William Tecumseh Sherman**.*

Led by a robed figure of **Victory** waving an olive branch, the monument is conceded to be perhaps the nation's finest equestrian statue.

Reminiscent of the clock tower at Venice's Piazza San Marco, the bell statue at **Herald Square** stands sentry over the distinctly New York scene of shoppers at Broadway and 34th Street.

Another American and New York hero dominates a long, narrow strip of park land that runs along the Hudson River on the city's Upper West Side. **Ulysses S. Grant**, the victorious Civil War general and beloved 18th President of the United States, is entombed with his wife here in one of the more somber-looking monuments in the city. A massive granite structure, **Grant's Tomb** was completed in 1897, sixteen years after his death, but not without the objections of neighbors who felt it would lend an undesirable funereal mood to the area. Instead however, it became a popular gathering place and to this day is the scene of annual memorial services with all the pomp reserved for a President.

Spanning the East River, **Manhattan Bridge** *with the* **Brooklyn Bridge** *in the background.*

Also known as the 59th Street Bridge , the **Queensboro Bridge,** *joins Manhattan to* **Long Island City** *in Queens.*

New Yorkers have a love-hate relationship with their bridges. They are loved for their beauty as marvels of engineering, but reviled for traffic congestion. To say the bridges and tunnels of **New York** are continuously busy would be an understatement. Each business day, they carry five million commuters to and from their work places in Manhattan by car, by cab, by bus and by train. Thousands more cross the harbor on the venerable **Staten Island Ferry**.

By evening, the congestion and jangled nerves of commuting dissolve into awe, especially in Brooklyn where the **Brooklyn Bridge** occupies the foreground of a glittering vista that is perhaps the most breathtaking view of night and the city. Further upstream on the East River, the **Manhattan Bridge** and the **Queensboro Bridge** serve as vital commuter links. The **Verrazano Bridge** which joins Queens with Staten Island is the traditional starting point for the annual New York marathon.

The **Verrazano Bridge** was named after the Italian explorer who discovered New York Bay in 1524.

Still thought by many to be the worlds most beautiful bridge, the **Brooklyn Bridge** was completed in 1883.

New York's theaters are as diverse in character and personality as its people., its neighborhoods, and its businesses. They can be sophisticated yet tawdry, artistic yet borderline commercial, insular yet eager for approval. As nowhere else on earth there is theater for every taste and pocketbook. The prestigious **Metropolitan Opera House**, formerly the elite preserve of tuxedo and pearls set, now reaches out to the working people, students, and tourists. Tickets are sold worldwide and many of the best seats are reserved for years. In contrast, some very trendy back alley off Broadway theaters with stark yet interesting interiors provide marvellous, innovative musicals and thrillers, especially attractive to the t-shirt and jean crowd. Between these extremes come the mega-musicals, experimental and popular, sure fire hits.

New Yorkers and visitors never tire of the lavish offerings at **Radio City Music Hall**. It's Christmas spectacular is one of the highlights of the holiday season.

Nowhere else on earth are the multiple personalities of a city routinely played out with such energy and elan as on the **New York stages**.

Radio City Music Hall.

Metropolitan Opera House at Lincoln Center for the Performing Arts.

Christmas spectacular decorations at **Radio City Music Hall**.

The venerable **Carnegie Hall**.

New York's *Theater District.*

Practically a fixture, **Cats** *at the Winter Garden.*

Shubert Theater in the heart of the theater district.

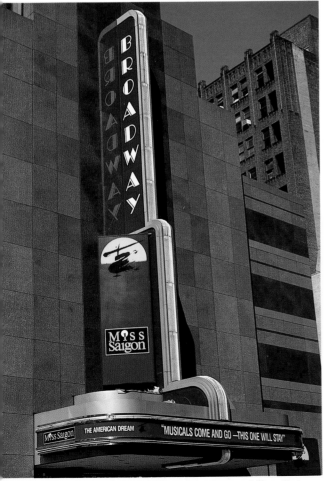

Complete with helicopter on stage, Miss Saigon.

If the essence of **New York** is captured in the theater, then to sample the offerings of **Broadway** must be the ultimate **New York** experience. And it seems visitors and New Yorkers alike cannot get enough quality theater. On Broadway, the success of a major musical is measured not in the number of weeks of sold out performances, but rather in the number of years. And while even the shortest run on Broadway is a sign of success in theater, many excellent plays are staged elsewhere in **New York**. "**Off Broadway**" and "**Off Off Broadway**" are terms given for artistic and economic, as well as the obvious geographic reasons. And with a little investigation, the adventurous theater-goers will discover future stars and Broadway-bound productions on some of the smaller, funkier stages off Broadway.

A Knickerbocker's game at Madison Square Garden.

Logo for the home team of Yankee Stadium.

When a New Yorker offers a visit to "**The Garden**", he isn't talking about flowers, unless there's a flower show at **Madison Square Garden**. With seating for 20,000 it's the largest indoor arena in New York and home for the **New York Knicks** of basketball and the **New York Rangers** of hockey. Uptown, in the Bronx, the **New York Yankees** baseball club plays its home games at the most storied facility in American sports, **Yankee Stadium**. Also in the Bronx is a contender for real and gorgeous gardens: the **New York Botanical Gardens** provide 250 acres of part unspoiled woodland along a winding river, part formal gardens, and a conservatory and arboretum. Another interesting garden is the **Sculpture Garden** at midtown's **Museum of Modern Art** which affords a tiny but beautiful rest spot amongst the office towers of Manhattan.

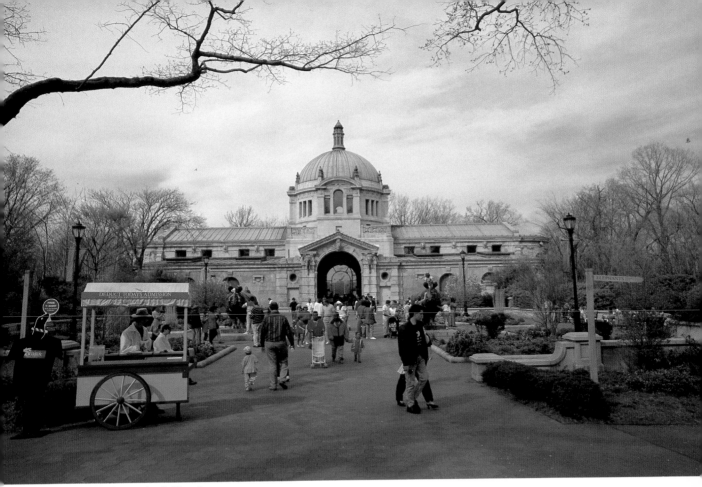

New York Botanical Gardens.

Museum of Modern Art's Sculpture Garden.

*The Cadillac's back end poised over the inevitable lineups at the **Hard Rock Cafe**.*

In a city of 15,000 **restaurants** it requires little imagination to understand how fierce competition has driven **New York** to its lofty position as the dining capital of the world. Nowhere in the world does the prospective diner have a greater selection of cuisines. Beyond the obvious delights of Chinatown and sushi bars of midtown, one can find exotic tastes in profusion. Brazilian, Indian, Ethiopian or Lebanese restaurants to name just a few, can be found in their respective neighborhoods competing with several others of identical ethnic origin. And, whether on the lookout for a gigantic pastrami sandwich, the perfect New York steak, or a classic American hamburger, the search for good American cuisine will not be a long one. In recent years, theme restaurants such as **"The Hard Rock Cafe"** and **"Planet Hollywood"** have adopted themes, displaying rock music and film memorabilia to attract customers in an increasingly competitive marketplace.

Harry Archer on the waterfront.

From the days of the first settlers, **the waterfront** was **New York's** traditional hub of trade and commerce. Fisherman and merchant mariners brought fish, produce, meat and other goods to an East River trading post at the foot of Fulton St., and in 1822 the **Fulton Street Market** was opened. It was New York's first waterfront market and remains a center of commerce to this day the main fish market for retailers and restaurants. In the mid-1960's, concerned citizens began work to save the old port which had fallen into disrepair as the shipping industry moved from Manhattan to Brooklyn and New Jersey. Many of the 19th century buildings had miraculously survived intact, albeit somewhat decayed, providing the framework for a renaissance of **New York's** historic waterfront.

Today the **South St. Seaport** is the focal point for a revived and thriving waterfront scene which includes pedestrian malls, a boardwalk, restored tall ships, restaurants, pubs and street performances. As always , the waterfront springs to life before dawn when the rejuvenated **Fulton St. Fish Market** opens for the sale of fresh fish brought to port. A restored old paddle-wheeler offers a ninety minute waterfront tour of the downtown area originating from its berth at South St. Seaport.

*The boardwalk along the waterfront at the south end of **Manhattan**.*

*The **South Street Seaport** at Pier 17.*

*"Transportation" sculpture group on the exterior of **Grand Central Station**.*

In the golden age of rail travel, the center of New York, for travellers, was undoubtedly **Grand Central Terminal**. Built in the Renaissance style of architecture and taking more than a dozen years to complete in 1913, Grand Central was immediately recognized as a masterpiece of engineering. Whether travelling for business or pleasure , any visitor's first steps in the city were almost always in Grand Central Terminal. Today it is busier than ever, overtaken by the rush of commuters using the subway and commuter trains from the outlying suburbs of **New York** and Connecticut.

◄ *Interior of the **Grand Central Station** during rush hour.*

For anyone who thinks they know **New York** there is always more whether it be the antique and crystal shops of **Soho**, the precious art galleries of **Thompson St.** or the after-hours blues bars of **Bleecker St**. A brisk autumn afternoon or a sweet spring morning can be spent taking in the scene at **Washington Square** park in **Greenwich Village** or haggling over fish prices on **Canal St.** in **Chinatown**. Either participating in the frenetic **New York** lifestyle or simply watching the passing parade, one always knows that around the next corner there is bound to be something interesting to see or do in **New York** the city that has it all.

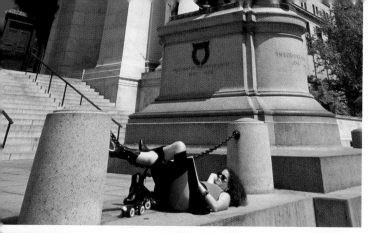

There are countless points of interest in this capital city of excitement, but its crowning and most endearing attraction is its people. New Yorkers stand alone among Americans for their diversity, their habits, their ingenuity, their clothes, their intensity, and their humor. They are the sons and daughters of every corner of the globe, each bringing his or her own special something to add to a city that is nothing if not a melting pot for all the cultures of the world.

*A wide lens aerial shot of all 5 boroughs of the city of **New York**.* ➤

Published and Distributed by
New York Souvenir Company

(A division of Irving Weisdorf & Co., Ltd.)
2801 John Street,
Markham, Ontario, L3R 2Y8

Text by
Mia Forbes/Harry Phillips

Designed by
David Villavera

Computer layout by
Amy Morrison

Photographer	Page
L. Fisher	Back cover, 1, 2, 3, 4/5, 6, 7a, 9, 10a, 11, 12, 14, 15, 17b, 18, 19, 22a, 23, 26, 27, 31, 33a, 34, 35, 36, 37, 38a, 39b, 40c, 41a, 42, 43a, 43c, 44, 45b, 48, 49c, 52, 54, 55a, 57, 58c, 60b, 60d, 60e, 60f, 60g, 61e, 61f
Forbes/Phillips	17a, 24a, 25a, 30b, 39a, 40a, 41b, 43b, 46a, 49a, 50b, 51a, 53a, 53c, 53e, 55b, 56, 58a, 59b, 59c, 60h, 61b, 61c
G. Kalinsky	50a
New York Visitors & Convention Bureau	13a, 32a, 33b, 38b, 45a, 46b, 47b
G. Romany	7b, 8, 10b, 13b, 16, 20/21, 22b, 32b, 40b, 47a, 49b, 53b, 53d, 58b, 60a, 60c, 61a
D. Villavera	30a, 51b, 61d

Printed in Canada